# Past and Present

*Jeri Freedman*

rosen publishing's
rosen central®

New York

Published in 2010 by The Rosen Publishing Group, Inc.
29 East 21st Street, New York, NY 10010

Copyright © 2010 by The Rosen Publishing Group, Inc.

First Edition

**Library of Congress Cataloging-in-Publication Data**

Freedman, Jeri.
Iowa: past and present / Jeri Freedman.—1st ed.
    p. cm.—(The United States: past and present)
Includes bibliographical references and index.
ISBN 978-1-4358-3517-7 (library binding)
ISBN 978-1-4358-8485-4 (pbk)
ISBN 978-1-4358-8484-7 (6 pack)
1. Iowa—Juvenile literature. I. Title.
F621.3.F74 2010
977.7—dc22

                                                                    2009024564

*Manufactured in the United States of America*

CPSIA Compliance Information: Batch #LW10YA: For Further Information contact Rosen Publishing, New York, New York at 1-800-237-9932

**On the cover:** Top left: An illustration of Lewis and Clark meeting Native Americans in Iowa. Top right: Iowa voters attend a Democratic caucus in Slater, Iowa. Bottom: An Iowa cornfield.

# Contents

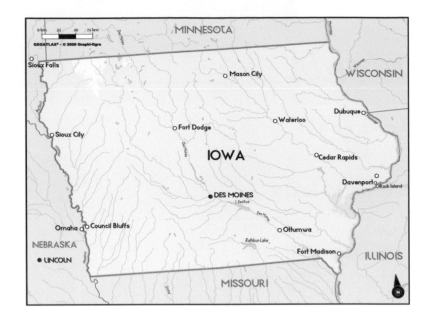

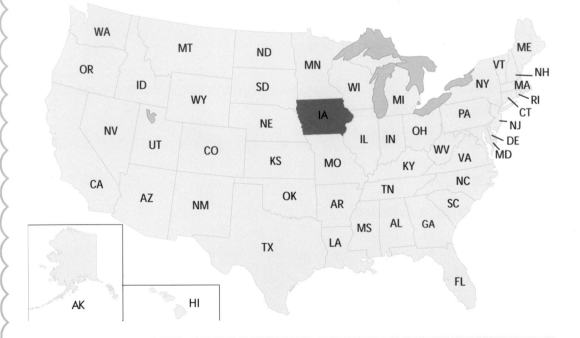

A state rich in farmland, Iowa is in the middle of the region of the United States known as the Midwest. Its capital, Des Moines, is located in the center of the state.

# Introduction

**Iowa** is located in the Midwestern part of the United States near the center of the country, an area often referred to as "America's Heartland." Iowa gets its name from the Ioway, a Native American tribe encountered by the first European settlers. On the west, the state is separated from Nebraska and South Dakota by the Missouri River. It is bordered by Minnesota to the north. The Mississippi River separates it from Wisconsin and Illinois to the east, and it is bordered by the state of Missouri to the south.

Iowa covers roughly 57,000 square miles (92,000 square kilometers), and has a population of approximately three million people. Many of the people living in Iowa today are descendents of immigrants from northern Europe who arrived during the late nineteenth and early twentieth centuries. Iowa's population is 90 percent white non-Hispanic, 2.6 percent African American, 1.6 percent Asian, and 4 percent Hispanic/Latino.

The rich topsoil of Iowa covers a layer of varied mineral deposits left by the glaciers that moved down from the north after the last ice age. Iowa's geologic past has given it a varied terrain. It has always been primarily an agricultural state. Part of the central "bread basket" of the United States, Iowa is a major producer of corn, soybeans, and hogs.

# Chapter 1

# THE LAND OF IOWA

**Millions** of years ago, Iowa was covered by a shallow sea. Ancient aquatic creatures lived in this sea. When these creatures died, their shells drifted to the bottom. Over millions of years, the level of the land rose. The sand of the sea bottom was compressed into sandstone and the shells into limestone. These materials form the bedrock that underlies Iowa today. There is also a great deal of coal in the ground in Iowa, formed from ancient trees and plants that died over the course of millions of years.

The Midcontinent Rift, which extends from Lake Superior to Kansas, runs through Iowa. A rift is an opening in the earth that formed when rocks split apart. The Midcontinent Rift, which is also called the Keweenawan Rift, is a chasm that formed 1.1 billion years ago when the continental plate that forms the United States split apart. Another notable geologic feature is the Manson Crater, which is located in Pocahontas County in the northwestern part of the state, near the city of Manson. This crater, which is about 1 mile (1.6 km) across, was formed when an asteroid crashed into the earth about seventy-four million years ago. There is little evidence of the crater visible today because glaciers moving south after the Ice Age filled it in with soil and rock.

West Okoboji Lake is located in northwest Iowa. Part of the Iowa Great Lakes, it is a popular destination for boating, fishing, and swimming.

## Geography of Modern Iowa

After the Ice Age, glaciers in Iowa traveled south as they melted. The glaciers dragged boulders and soil with them. The boulders and rocks were covered with clay, loam, and loess (a yellow mix of sand, soil, and clay, which is formed by erosion). These boulders carved valleys into the terrain.

Iowa contains several different types of terrain. In the extreme northeast corner of the state is the Paleozoic Plateau, which extends down from Wisconsin. It contains bedrock outcroppings and deep

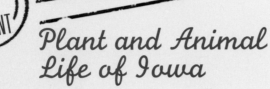

## Plant and Animal Life of Iowa

Ten thousand years ago, Iowa was a very different environment than it is today. The climate was colder and wetter. Northern-central Iowa was covered by forests, and there was very little prairie compared to today. From 9500 to 7500 BCE, Iowa was inhabited by Paleo-Indians (prehistoric ancestors of today's Native Americans). These people were hunters who constantly moved from one place to another. Many of the animals they hunted are now extinct. Their prey included mastodons, mammoths, and giant bison, which they hunted with stone-tipped weapons.

Today, the eastern and southern parts of the state are home to forests of deciduous (leaf-shedding) trees, including oaks, silver maples, and cottonwoods. Gooseberry and wild grape grow in areas with rivers. The animals in Iowa today, including raccoons, rabbits, beavers, muskrats, deer, and otters, are smaller than those of ten thousand years ago. Wild turkeys are native to Iowa, and although they were extinct in the state at one time, they were successfully reintroduced in the 1970s. As Iowa developed prairies, it became home to such birds as prairie chickens, grouse, and bobolinks. Another bird that has returned to the state is the bald eagle, which spends winters there.

Iowa's prairies are also home to animals that include badgers and gophers, which build their burrows in the soft soil. Many plants and animals migrated from farther south along the Des Moines River into the Des Moines River Valley, and up the Missouri and Mississippi rivers. Among these are sycamore trees, which have only been present in Iowa for the last one hundred years, and ducks, geese, pelicans, and sandhill cranes. According to the Iowa Department of Natural Resources, the Northwest Iowa Plains region "is the highest and driest region of the Western Corn Belt Plains."

river valleys. Directly to the west of this area is the Iowa Surface, an area of gently rolling plains formed by erosion and dotted with boulders. A section of hills extends from the northwest to the southeast across the plains of the Iowa Surface. The large central portion of the state forms the Des Moines Lobe. This area was formed between twelve thousand and fifteen thousand years ago by glaciers, and it's filled with knobby hills and wetlands. Along the western edge of this area are three major lakes: Spirit Lake, East Okoboji Lake, and West Okoboji Lake. These are the largest natural lakes in Iowa and are known as the Iowa Great Lakes.

A young bison stands with its mother at the Neal Smith National Wildlife Refuge in Iowa. The preserve is home to free-ranging buffalo.

Below the Des Moines Lobe area, extending across the southern part of the state, is the Southern Iowa Drift Plain. This part of the state was formed by deposits left by glaciers about half a million years ago. Numerous rivers and streams run through this area, carving out hills and valleys. Along the left edge of the Southern Iowa Drift Plain are the Loess Hills.

Along the eastern and western edges of the state are plains formed by river silt deposited by the Mississippi and Missouri rivers, respectively. The final type of terrain is the Northwest Iowa Plains, extending from the Missouri River through the Big Sioux River Valley. It is an area of rolling hills with a higher elevation and drier climate than other parts of Iowa. This area is notable for its exposed reddish quartzite, which is the oldest bedrock in the state, at 1.6 billion years old.

# Climate

Iowa has hot summers, wet springs, and cold winters. The average annual temperature is 49 degrees Fahrenheit (9 degrees Celsius). In the center of the state, temperatures typically range from a high of 86°F (30°C) in July to a low of 10°F (−4°C) in January. Annual precipitation (rain and snowfall) averages 34.7 inches (88 centimeters), and annual snowfall is about 30 inches (76 cm). Iowa ranks sixth among the states for frequency of tornadoes.

# Major Cities

Iowa has a number of major cities. Des Moines, Iowa's largest city, is the state capital. It has a population of nearly two hundred thousand, and a metropolitan-area population of around five hundred thousand. Founded in 1857, the city is named after the Des Moines River on which it sits. "Des Moines" is a shortened form of *Rivière des Moines*, which is French for "River of the Monks." There is a debate over whether "the monks" refers to the monks who lived near the river, the local Moingana tribe, or if it is a corruption of the French word for "middle" (*de moyen*), because it sits between the Missouri and Mississippi rivers. About 30 miles (48.3 km) from Des Moines is the city of Ames, which is home to Iowa State University.

Iowa City is located on the Iowa River in Johnson County. Iowa City was the first capital of Iowa when it became a state in 1846. It is also home to the University of Iowa.

Davenport is a city of about one hundred thousand people in Scott County on the Mississippi River. It was founded by Antoine LeClaire in 1836, following the end of the Black Hawk War in 1832. Antoine named the town Davenport in honor of his friend Colonel George Davenport.

Dubuque is another city on the Mississippi River. It is the site of one of the oldest settlements west of the Mississippi River. It was settled by Julien Dubuque in 1785. Today, it is a major manufacturing center.

Sioux City has a population of about eighty-five thousand people and is

Here is the skyline of Des Moines. The tall building in the center is 801 Grand. It's the largest building in Iowa.

located in the western part of the state at the head of the Missouri River. Originally settled by the Sioux tribe, it is now home to four colleges: Morningside College, Briar Cliff University, St. Luke's College, and Western Iowa Tech Community College.

# Chapter 2

# THE HISTORY OF IOWA

Native Americans have lived in Iowa since prehistoric times. The earliest Native Americans are simply known as the Mound Builders. They lived all through the Mississippi River Valley. Today, the only traces of them are the mounds that they left behind. Some were used for burials and contain artifacts such as weapons and drawings of animals, many of which are now extinct. Some were built in the shapes of animals and may have had a ceremonial purpose.

## Early History

By the time European traders came to the region in the late 1600s, it was already inhabited by two major groups of Native Americans: Algonquins, who had migrated west from the Great Lakes, and the Sioux (also called the Eastern Dakotas), who had migrated from the Rocky Mountains. The Ioway Indians in southern Iowa were a branch of the Dakotas, as were the Winnebagos. The Potawatomi, Ottawa, and Chippewa were tribes of the Algonquin branch of Native Americans.

The most powerful tribes in the Mississippi River area were the Sac (or Sauk) and Mesquakie, which means "fox." In 1804, the U.S.

government made a treaty with these tribes, in which they signed away all of their land in Illinois and agreed to move west of the Mississippi River. Many of the Sac disagreed with the treaty, however, and in 1831, Chief Black Hawk refused to vacate the area. Chief Black Hawk led a rebellion but was captured and imprisoned. The tribe was forced to give up more of their land west of the Mississippi.

The first European explorers to reach Iowa were Louis Joliet (1645–1700) and Father Jacques Marquette (1637–1675), who was a Catholic priest. These two Frenchmen traveled from eastern Canada down the St. Lawrence River and across the Great Lakes.

This 1844 painting, titled *Female War Eagle, Iowa Tribe,* is by the artist George Catlin (1796–1872).

They sailed down the Mississippi River from Wisconsin through Iowa, all the way to the Gulf of Mexico. Nine years later, King Louis XIV (1638–1715) of France sent a man named René-Robert Cavelier, Sieur de La Salle (1643–1687), to sail the entire length of the Mississippi, claiming all of the land he traveled through for France. He named the area Louisiana in honor of King Louis.

In 1803, President Thomas Jefferson (1743–1826) purchased the entire French holdings in North America for $15 million. This transaction is known as the Louisiana Purchase. In 1804, President

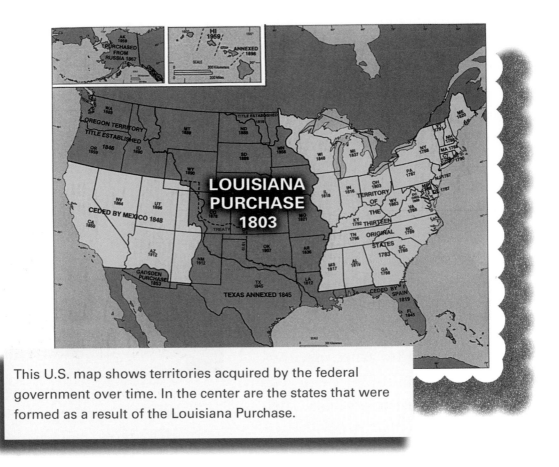

This U.S. map shows territories acquired by the federal government over time. In the center are the states that were formed as a result of the Louisiana Purchase.

Jefferson sent an expedition headed by Captain Meriwether Lewis and Lieutenant William Clark up the Missouri River to explore the territory that it ran through, including part of Iowa.

# The Nineteenth Century

In the 1800s, the U.S. government opened Iowa to settlers, who set up farms on the rich prairie. By 1870, Iowa had a population of nearly one million people. Most of the settlers who arrived in Iowa prior to 1865 came from the northeastern, midwestern, and southern parts of the United States. After 1865, significant numbers of immigrants started settling in Iowa. They mostly came from places in northern Europe, including England, France, Germany, and Scandinavia. These immigrants were looking for cheap land that they could farm.

Over time, the land acquired in the Louisiana Purchase was divided up into territories. These territories gradually became states. Until 1821, Iowa was part of the Missouri Territory. When Missouri became a state in 1821, Iowa was left as an unorganized territory. It was closed to new settlers until 1834, when it was made part of the Michigan Territory. When Michigan received statehood in 1836, Iowa and Wisconsin became the Wisconsin Territory. In 1838, Iowa became the Iowa Territory, and finally, in 1846, it achieved statehood.

## Building the Railroad

By the 1850s, railroads were revolutionizing transportation in the United States. Railroads allowed people to travel back and forth between the East Coast and the Midwest. They also enabled goods to be quickly and easily transported.

People in Iowa wanted to form railroad companies to connect to the railroads that linked the East Coast and Illinois. This would allow them to transport farm products from Iowa to the East Coast, and possibly also ship them from the East Coast to Europe. In 1856, the U.S. government gave land grants of 4 million acres (1,618,742 hectares) to railroad companies in Iowa, which they could sell to raise money for construction. The railroad companies in Iowa at that time were the Chicago and North Western, the Rock Island, the Illinois Central, and the Burlington. The Illinois Central later merged with the Dubuque and Pacific Railroad to form one company.

# Life on the Prairie

Early settlers in Iowa lived in a type of housing known as log cabins. However, in grassy areas like northwest Iowa, where trees were scarce, they built sod houses. These houses were made of sod, which is the grass-covered surface of the ground.

Because prairies have few trees, it was possible to set up farms in the 1800s without having to clear forests beforehand. Land was farmed by using horse-drawn or ox-drawn plows, and crops were harvested by hand. But the lack of trees also meant that there was little wood available to build houses with. There were some trees along the rivers that people could use. Nevertheless, many of the first settlers in Iowa lived in sod houses.

To make sod houses, settlers cut brick-shaped chunks of sod from the prairie. The sod consisted of clumps of earth held together by the matted roots of strong grasses, such as buffalograss and wiregrass. The sod bricks formed the walls of the house. As the sod walls were built up, windows and door frames were inserted. These windows and door frames were held in place by pegs. Roofs were made of sod and tar paper placed over wooden rafters.

Another type of sod house was constructed by digging out a hill. This type of sod house was called a dugout. Living in a sod house, no matter how it was constructed, was not very comfortable. They were, as might be expected, damp and often muddy when it rained.

Living on the prairie, there was little wood for fuel. People burned corncobs, dried cow patties (cow manure), and knots of dried prairie grass in their fireplaces. It was the children's job to tie the prairie grass into knots. Eventually, settlers discovered coal in Iowa, and they found that it could be used for fuel.

Today's Iowans live in modern wood-frame houses. Heat is provided by oil or natural gas, and gas-powered tractors and automated farm machines are used to plant and harvest crops.

Iowa's railroads successfully connected to those extending to the east. The Illinois Central, which began its route in Chicago, would eventually extend across Nebraska to meet the Union Pacific Railroad coming from California. When this occurred, Iowa was tied into a system of railroads that stretched from coast to coast.

# Iowa in the Civil War

When Iowa joined the Union in 1846, it declared itself a free state—one where slavery was not allowed. During the Civil War (1861–1865), seventy thousand soldiers from Iowa fought on the side of the Union. Iowan regiments fought in battles in Shiloh, Tennessee; Vicksburg, Mississippi; and Atlanta and Savannah, Georgia. Iowan women bought or made supplies needed by the soldiers, including medicine and bullets. They shipped supplies by steamboat down the Mississippi River.

Iowa was also a stop on the Underground Railroad, a network of abolitionists (people who wanted to end slavery) across the country who helped slaves escape to places where they could be free. Participants in the Underground Railroad in Iowa helped slaves escape from the South to Canada.

This illustration depicts the Iowan regiment in the Battle of Wilson's Creek, Missouri, which took place on August 10, 1861.

# Iowa During World War I

World War I (1914–1918) started in 1914, when Archduke Franz Ferdinand of Austria was assassinated. The assassination of the archduke sent shockwaves across Europe, and soon countries were mobilizing for a full-out war. At the time, Austria was an ally of Germany. France, Russia, and Britain fought against Germany, Austria, and their allies.

The United States officially entered World War I in 1917. About 114,000 Iowans served in the military during the war and 3,576 died. Camp Dodge was built northwest of Des Moines for the training of soldiers. It became the first training center in the United States to accept African American soldiers. Because the military was segregated at that time, black and white soldiers lived and trained separately.

Women also participated in the war as nurses, as ambulance drivers, and in other support positions. Marian Crandall (1872–1918) was born in Cedar Rapids and taught French at St. Katherine's School in Davenport. During the war, Crandall went to France. There, she worked in the canteen, where soldiers were fed. She was the first woman killed in the war, when an artillery shell hit the canteen.

During World War I, there was a lot of prejudice against German Americans. Many people in Iowa had German ancestry and were treated harshly. Some were required to take a loyalty oath to the United States. Schools also stopped teaching German, and terms with "German" in them were changed: for example, German measles became "liberty measles."

# The Great Depression in Iowa

During the war, the demand for massive quantities of food to feed the troops led to high prices and prosperity for Iowan farmers. After

This photo shows an Iowan family during the Great Depression. Having no money, they are preparing to sell their possessions and trailer so that they can buy food.

the war, prices dropped as demand decreased. This caused financial hardship for many farmers. In 1929, the situation became significantly worse. This was the year that the United States entered a decade-long economic downturn known as the Great Depression.

The Great Depression began with the stock market crash of October 29, 1929. Banks that had lent huge sums of money to investors who could not repay it did not have enough money to cover the deposits that their customers had put into their accounts. People rushed to take their money out of banks. As a result, banks ran out of money and failed. Unable to borrow money to buy materials and pay employees, many businesses also failed. At the height of the Great Depression, unemployment in the United States reached 25 percent.

During the Great Depression, prices for farm products dropped. As farmers in Iowa made less money, many couldn't pay the mortgages on their farms. Eventually, they lost their land. When Franklin D. Roosevelt (1882–1945) became president in 1933, he implemented a series of programs called the New Deal. These programs were designed to stimulate the economy. One of the acts passed as part of the New Deal was the Agricultural Adjustment Act. Under this act, the U.S. government attempted to shore up prices for agricultural products by renting land from farmers but not growing anything on it. This provided the farmers with some additional income, while also reducing the supply of produce. A smaller supply meant that farmers could charge higher prices for their produce.

# Iowa During World War II

At the end of World War I, Germany was forced to sign the Treaty of Versailles, in which it gave up much of its territory. In the following years, Germany suffered a serious depression of its own. In 1933, Adolf Hitler came to power in Germany, promising to revive the country as a world power. In 1939, Germany invaded Poland and began World War II, a war that involved most of the world's nations. Germany and its allies were known as the Axis Powers.

In December 1941, Japan, a member of the Axis Powers, carried out a surprise attack on the American naval fleet stationed at Pearl

Harbor, Hawaii. The United States entered the war on the side of the Allies, which included Britain, France, and Russia.

Nearly 8,400 Iowans were killed in World War II. The U.S. Air Force built a number of air bases in Iowa to train pilots and crews of fighter planes and bombers. The Women's Auxiliary Army Corps (WAACs) was established during the war, allowing women to join the U.S. military for the first time. The first training center for WAACs was established in Des Moines, under the command of Colonel Mildred McAfee Horton.

In a wartime tragedy, five brothers from an Iowan family, the Sullivans, were killed while serving on the same ship. This led to the enforcement of the rule against brothers serving in the same unit and to the implementation of the Sole Survivor Rule by the military. Under this rule, once one or more members of a family have been killed in combat, other members of that family are protected from the draft and from serving in combat positions.

# Chapter 3

# THE GOVERNMENT OF IOWA

**Iowa** is divided into ninety-nine counties. The state government consists of three branches: the executive branch, the legislative branch, and the judicial branch. The government is located in the capital city, Des Moines. Iowa is governed by a group of laws known as the Code of Iowa.

## The Executive Branch

The highest official in state government is the governor. The governor is responsible for overseeing the administration of the state. Second in command to the governor is the lieutenant governor.

A number of other officials also play key roles in administering the affairs of the state. The secretary of state is responsible for a number of duties, including overseeing voter registration, the insurance commission, state records, and elections. The state auditor monitors the state's financial records to ensure that money is spent properly. The treasurer is responsible for collecting taxes and overseeing the state's funds. The attorney general is in charge of the legal affairs of the state and prosecuting those who violate laws.

The secretary of agriculture is the head of the four-hundred-person Iowa Department of Agriculture. The department is responsible for issues relating to land and farming. Its programs include protecting waterways and dealing with issues such as land erosion. It also provides programs to assist farmers.

## The Legislative Branch

The formal name of the Iowa Legislature is the Iowa General Assembly. Like the U.S. Congress, the Iowa Legislature consists of two houses: a Senate and a House of Representatives. The Senate consists of fifty members, one elected from each of Iowa's

This portrait of Robert Lucas hangs in the Iowa statehouse. President Martin Van Buren appointed Lucas governor of the Iowa Territory in 1838.

fifty districts. Each senatorial district is divided into two congressional districts, from which members are elected to the House of Representatives. Thus, there are one hundred members in the House of Representatives. Senators are elected to four-year terms and representatives to two-year terms.

## The Judicial Branch

The court system in Iowa is divided into two types of courts: district courts, where trials are held, and appellate courts, which review

# Iowa's Government

Before becoming a state in 1846, Iowa was first a district, and then a territory. A territory is governed differently than a state. As a district and a territory, Iowa was the property of the federal government. A district is an area that has few settlers. As a district, Iowa was managed by a district governor. The governor was appointed by the president of the United States. The governor used army troops to protect the settlers.

When enough settlers arrived, Iowa became a territory. Settlers in a territory had more say in governing themselves than people in a district—but less than citizens of states. The governor of the territory was still appointed by the president; the people had no say in who was chosen. They also had no representatives in Congress to speak for their interests. However, they were allowed to elect their own territorial legislature and pass laws that governed how affairs were carried out within the territory. The first governor of the Iowa Territory was Robert Lucas, who was appointed by President Martin Van Buren in 1838. A secretary, chief justice (judge), two associate justices, a U.S. attorney, and a federal marshal were also provided for the Iowa Territory by the federal government.

Iowa's territorial legislature had two houses: the Council, which had thirteen members elected for two years, and the House of Representatives, which had twenty-six members elected for one year. Although the governor had chosen Burlington as his seat of office, the legislature felt that it was too inaccessible. At their insistence, a new capital was set up on the Iowa River. It was called Iowa City.

On December 28, 1846, Iowa became the twenty-ninth state in the Union. Statehood gave the citizens the same rights to self-government that those in all U.S. states enjoy. Today, Iowans can elect their own governor and state officials, as well as their own legislature. Iowa has two senators, like all states, and five congressmen in the U.S. House of Representatives.

court decisions. There are two types of appellate courts. The first is the state supreme court, which rules on whether court decisions and actions of the executive branch are constitutional. The second is appeals courts, which review the verdicts of district courts when necessary. The supreme court has seven justices and is the highest court in the state.

The state capitol building in Des Moines was built between 1871 and 1886. The dome is covered with gold leaf.

## The Iowa Caucuses

Iowa plays an important role in presidential elections. The state holds the first presidential caucuses. Caucuses are meetings of voters who select delegates to state Republican and Democratic conventions. The caucuses are currently held in January of an election year. Because Iowans make the first choice of both the Republican and Democratic candidates, they have become the focus of massive media attention as the race for the presidential nomination begins.

# Chapter 4

# THE ECONOMY OF IOWA

Iowa's most important industry is agriculture. According to the 2007 Census of Agriculture produced by the U.S. Census Bureau, there are an estimated 92,700 farms in Iowa, covering approximately 31.7 million acres (12.8 million hectares).

Iowa is the nation's top producer of corn and soybeans. In 2007, Iowa's farmers grew 2.4 billion bushels of corn. In addition to being used as food for both humans and animals, corn is now used to produce the alternative fuel ethanol. Iowan farmers also produced 439 million bushels of soybeans in 2007. Iowa has about four million head of cattle and marketed 3.6 million head of cattle in 2007. There are also roughly two hundred thousand head of dairy cattle in the state. Iowa has about 19.3 million hogs, and it sold about 47.3 million in 2007. In addition, it sold about 10.3 million chickens. Iowa's total farm-related income in 2007 was approximately $20.4 billion.

Given the importance of agriculture to Iowa's economy, it is not surprising that a variety of companies producing agricultural-related products have developed in the state. One such company is Deere & Company (also known as John Deere), which makes tractors and farm equipment. Although it is now headquartered in Moine, Illinois, the company started in Waterloo, Iowa, in 1918. Today, Deere is one of the largest manufacturers of farm equipment worldwide. Other

Cornfields like this one are a common sight in Iowa. Agriculture has always been important to the state, which is a key part of the United States' "bread basket."

Iowa companies with products related to agriculture include Pioneer Hi-Bred International, a division of DuPont that provides research and development services for genetically modifying plants, and Terra Industries, Inc., a major fertilizer producer. Other major agricultural product companies operating in the state include Cargill, Monsanto, Ajinomoto, Rose Acre Farms, Hy-line International, Garst

# Mining in Iowa

At one time, Iowa had a booming mining industry, with its large deposits of coal, lead, and other minerals. Coal mining in Iowa became big business in the 1880s, when the construction of the railroad made it possible to ship large quantities of coal across the country.

By 1900, there were four hundred coal mines in Iowa. All were shaft mines in which coal miners descended 250 feet (76.2 m) underground to mine the coal. The miners went down the shaft in elevators. They chopped the coal and removed it from the mines by mule-drawn carts. Miners were often killed in cave-ins and other such accidents. Competition from mines in other states ultimately reduced the demand for Iowan coal, and eventually, all of the mines shut down. In the 1980s, a few strip mines operated in the state. Strip mining is a process by which the soil is completely stripped off an area of land, and large machines remove the exposed coal. It is much less expensive than shaft mining, but it is also very bad for the environment.

Today, all of the coal mines in Iowa have been shut down. In fact, there are few mines left in Iowa. Minerals collected today primarily include limestone and gypsum, used for construction, as well as other industrial minerals.

This section from a fossilized tree was found in a coal mine in Pella, Iowa. Workers at the Smithsonian Museum of Natural History in Washington, D.C., are seen here preparing it for an exhibition. The fossil weighs 16.5 tons (15 metric tons).

Seed Company, and Heart-land Pork Enterprises.

## Manufacturing

Iowa is a leader in advanced manufacturing, which is the rapid introduction of new processes, materials, and technologies into manufacturing applications. These manufacturing companies are located in each of Iowa's ninety-nine counties. The most significant manufacturing industries are food processing, machinery for agriculture, construction, mining, and chemicals.

Approximately 16 percent of Iowa's workforce, or about 220,000 people, are employed in the manufac-

At this Archer Daniels Midland loading site, corn is being tested to make sure that it is safe. The corn will be processed and made into food products.

turing sector. In 2003, manufacturing contributed $20.8 billion to Iowa's gross state product (GSP), and amounts to almost 21 percent of Iowa's GSP. Well-known advanced manufacturing businesses in Iowa include 3M, Alcoa, Electrolux, John Deere, Lennox Manufacturing, the Maytag Corporation, Rockwell Collins, and Winnebago.

Workers at the Winnebago factory in Forest City, Iowa, install a floor in a motor home. Winnebago, Inc., is the largest manufacturer of motor homes in the United States.

Given the state's premiere position as an agricultural products producer, it's not surprising that food processing is the largest segment of the manufacturing industry. Food processing contributes more than $4.4 billion to Iowa's GSP, which is just over 21 percent of the manufacturing GSP of the state. There are nearly six hundred food industry businesses in Iowa, including ConAgra Foods, Wells Dairy, Interstate Bakeries (makers of Wonder bread), Barilla, and Heinz, among others.

# Biotechnology

Iowa has a rich history in the life sciences sector, and it's building a strong foundation in biotechnology. Iowa is home to more than 1,800 biotech establishments, ranging from large international companies to small start-ups. Many of the globally respected companies in this field are located in the state, including Wyeth Pharmaceuticals, Roche, Roquette, Boehringer Ingelheim, and Wacker. Iowa is also home to a large number of start-up companies that are working on developing new products in the biotechnology field.

# Insurance

Companies started providing insurance in Iowa as far back as the 1800s. Always in danger of prairie fires, floods, tornadoes, and other natural disasters, Iowans got together to form mutual insurance companies. In these companies, groups of people contributed funds to a pool that was used to reimburse members in the event of a loss.

One of the earliest commercial insurance companies was formed in 1879 by Edward Temple, a banker from Chariton, Iowa. The company was called Banker's Life Association. In 1979, when the company expanded into other financial services areas, such as investing, it changed its name to Principal Financial Group. Today, there are more than six thousand firms employing 81,000 people in this industry in Iowa. Des Moines is currently one of the top centers of the insurance industry in the country.

# PEOPLE FROM IOWA: PAST AND PRESENT

# Chapter 5

There have been many Iowans who have contributed to politics, science, the arts, entertainment, and other areas. From scientists such as Norman Borlaug, to social reformers such as Amelia Jenks Bloomer, to athletes such as Shawn Johnson, the people of Iowa have helped shape America.

## Politics and Social Causes

**Amelia Jenks Bloomer (1818–1894)** Bloomer's family moved to Iowa in 1852, and she lived in Council Bluffs. As head of the Iowa Women's Suffrage Union, she fought for women's right to vote. The loose-fitting pants called "bloomers" are named after her.

**Annie Turner Wittenmyer (1827–1927)** During the Civil War, Wittenmyer was a crusader for better food and conditions in Union military hospitals. In 1862, she was appointed sanitary (health) agent for the Iowa Sanitary Commission and was ultimately put in charge of the kitchens of all Union military hospitals. In 1898, she was granted a pension by Congress for her work.

**Viola Babcock Miller (1871–1937)** Born in Washington County, Miller was elected Iowa secretary of state in 1932. The first woman to hold that office, Miller was responsible for the establishment of the Iowa Highway Patrol in 1935.

**John L. Lewis (1880–1969)** Born in Cleveland, Iowa, Lewis was a labor leader, who organized the CIO (Congress of Industrial Organizations) in the 1930s and unionized coal miners and other industrial workers. He was the head of the United Mine Workers of America for forty years, from 1920–1960.

John L. Lewis, seen here in a 1922 photo, was a major labor leader in the United States.

# Scientists

**Norman Borlaug (1914– )** Born in the Norwegian American community of Saude near Cresco, Borlaug is considered the father of the "green revolution." He pioneered

Nobel Prize–winning biologist Dr. Norman Borlaug shows stalks of wheat that he crossbred to be disease-resistant. Borlaug's wheat was also capable of producing higher yields.

the development of high-yielding wheat to feed people worldwide. Bourlaug was awarded the Nobel Peace Prize in 1970.

**James A. Van Allen (1914–2006)** Born in Mount Pleasant, Van Allen was an astronomer who was the first to detect the radiation belts that surround the earth. These bands of electrically charged particles now bear his name (the Van Allen belt). They are held in place by the earth's magnetic field.

**Lee de Forest (1873–1961)** Born in Council Bluffs, de Forest was the inventor of the vacuum tube, a device that takes electronic signals and amplifies them. Vacuum tubes were used in early radios and televisions. De Forest's work paved the way for the electronics age.

**Glenn Martin (1886–1955)**  Born in Macksburg, Martin was an aviator and founder of the Glenn Martin Company, which manufactured airplanes. In 1961, the Glenn Martin Company merged with American-Marietta and became Martin Marietta. In 1995, Martin Marietta merged with Lockheed to become Lockheed-Martin.

# Arts and Entertainment

**Buffalo Bill (William) Cody (1846–1917)**  Born in Le Claire, Buffalo Bill began his careers as a soldier and buffalo hunter for the railroad. Later in life, Buffalo Bill achieved fame as a performer, touring the country with his traveling Wild West show.

**Grant Wood (1891–1942)**  Born in Anamosa, Wood was a painter of rural American scenes. He is best known for the painting *American Gothic*. Wood taught at the University of Iowa.

**George H. Gallup (1901–1984)**  Born Jefferson, Iowa, Gallup was a pioneer in developing statistical techniques for surveys of public opinion. He is the inventor of the famous Gallup Poll, which is often used to predict the outcome of elections. In 1958, Gallup formed the Gallup Organization, which still performs polls today on topics of social change

# The Amish of Iowa

The Amish are a group of people, primarily of German origin, who believe in maintaining a simple communal lifestyle. The largest and most well-known Amish communities are found in central Pennsylvania. The Amish originally emigrated from Germany to the United States in the 1800s. In the 1840s, some settled in the Midwest, including Iowa.

The first Amish bishop in Iowa was Jacob Swartzentruber. A German immigrant, Swartzentruber came to the United States in 1833. Initially, he settled in an Amish community in Somerset, Pennsylvania, and then moved to another in Maryland. In 1846, he relocated to Iowa with his family, but illness later forced him to return to Maryland. He longed to be in the new territories opening up in the West as they developed, however. And in 1851, he again returned to Iowa. He was recruited to be one of two ministers in the Amish community in Johnson County, Iowa. In 1869, Swartzentruber was ordained bishop of the Deer Creek district in Iowa.

As times changed, the Amish did not adopt modern inventions such as electricity. Their religious teachings said that they should live simply, in the same manner as they had in the past. Not all Amish agreed that embracing progress was wrong, however. In 1927, an Amish bishop named Moses M. Beachy (1874–1946) established a new congregation of Amish in Somerset County, Pennsylvania. This faction became known as the Beachy Amish.

Some members of the Amish community in Iowa adopted the Beachy Amish philosophy as well, setting up their own communities. Those following the traditional Amish lifestyle became known as the Old Order Amish. The lifestyle of the Old Order Amish in Iowa today has remained largely the same as it has been for years. The Amish dress in simple handmade clothes, farm with horses and plows, do not use electricity, and drive horses and buggies rather than automobiles. Today's Beachy Amish, in contrast, live in houses that have electricity and telephones, and they drive automobiles.

and political events. Gallup's home can still be seen in Jefferson.

**John Wayne (1907–1979)** Born Marion Robert Morrison in Winterset, but better known by his stage name, John Wayne, this actor was an iconic presence in American cinema. Wayne was best known for his roles in Westerns. In 1969, he won an Oscar for Best Actor for his work in the film *True Grit*.

**Robert William (Bob) Feller (1918– )** Raised in the town of Van Meter and dubbed the "Heater from Van Meter," Feller was a pitcher with the Cleveland Indians baseball team for eighteen years. In 1962, he was elected to the Baseball Hall of Fame.

Gymnast Shawn Johnson holds up her gold medal after the women's balance beam final at the 2008 Olympics in Beijing, China.

**Shawn Johnson (1992– )** Born in Des Moines, Johnson is a gymnast and Olympic medal winner. In the 2008 Olympics, she won a gold medal in the balance beam and a silver medal in the all-around gymnastics competition.

# Timeline

| | |
|---|---|
| **1673** | Louis Joliet and Father Jacques Marquette explore the area of Iowa along the Mississippi River for the king of France. |
| **1682** | La Salle claims Iowa as part of the Louisiana Territory in the name of the king of France. |
| **1803** | Thomas Jefferson acquires Iowa for the United States as part of the Louisiana Purchase. |
| **1804** | Lewis and Clark explore Iowa; the U.S. government acquires tribal lands from the Sac tribe. |
| **1812** | Iowa becomes part of the Missouri Territory when Louisiana becomes a state. |
| **1832** | After a military conflict called the Black Hawk War, the Sac tribe is forced to give up land in Iowa. |
| **1838** | Iowa becomes a stand-alone territory. |
| **1844** | The Iowa legislative assembly drafts a constitution. |
| **1846** | Iowa becomes a state. |
| **1856** | The federal government provides land grants to build railroads in Iowa. |
| **1862** | The Homestead Act allows people to settle on unoccupied land in Iowa. |
| **1867** | The first railroad in Iowa is completed. |
| **1913** | Keokuk Dam is built. |
| **1917** | Camp Dodge becomes a major training center for African American soldiers. |
| **1922** | The first woman is elected to public office in Iowa. |
| **1976** | The Iowa caucuses are established, enhancing Iowa's role in presidential elections. |
| **1993** | Flooding devastates Iowa. |
| **2008** | Flooding from the Mississippi River damages Cedar Rapids, Iowa; Iowa becomes the first state to choose Barack Obama as the Democratic nominee for president of the United States. |
| **2009** | Iowa legalizes same-sex marriage. |

# Iowa at a Glance

| | |
|---|---|
| **State motto** | "Our Liberties We Prize and Our Rights We Will Maintain" |
| **State capital** | Des Moines |
| **State tree** | Oak |
| **State flower** | Wild prairie rose (*Rosa pratincola*) |
| **State bird** | American goldfinch (*Carduelis tristis*) |
| **Statehood date and number** | 1846; the twenty-ninth state |
| **State nickname** | Hawkeye State |
| **Total area and U.S. rank** | 56,272 square miles (145, 744 sq km); twenty-fifth largest state |
| **Population** | 3 million |
| **Highest elevation** | 1,670 feet (509 m) in Sibley |
| **Lowest elevation** | The point where the Mississippi and Des Moines rivers meet: 480 feet (146 m) |

State Flag

State Seal

| Major rivers | Mississippi River, Missouri River, Des Moines River |
|---|---|
| Major lakes | Spirit Lake, East Okoboji Lake, West Okoboji Lake |
| Hottest temperature recorded | 118°F (48°C) at Keokuk, on July 20, 1934 |
| Coldest temperature recorded | –47°F (–44°C) at Washta, on January 12, 1912; and at Elkader, on February 3, 1996 |
| Origin of state name | Named after the Ioway Native American tribe |
| Chief agricultural products | Corn, dairy products, hogs, oats, soybeans |
| Major industries | Agriculture, fertilizer, food processing, insurance, manufacturing |

American goldfinch

Wild prairie rose

**abolitionist** A person dedicated to ending slavery.

**amplify** To make bigger or louder.

**canteen** A facility that serves food.

**communal property** Property shared by a group of people.

**continental plate** A sublayer of the earth's rocky crust.

**deciduous tree** A tree that sheds its leaves in the autumn.

**detainment** The act of arresting a person or holding that person against his or her will.

**geologic** Relating to the chemical and physical structure of the earth.

**glacier** A large sheet of ice.

**Ice Age** A period of extreme cold that occurred from two million to eleven thousand years ago.

**immigrate** To move to another country.

**loess** A yellow mix of sand, soil, and clay caused by the erosion of rock.

**magnetic field** A layer of magnetic force that surrounds the earth and is produced by molten metals rotating in the earth's core.

**migrate** To move from one place to another.

**Paleo-Indians** Prehistoric ancestors of present-day Native Americans.

**precipitation** Rain and snow.

**prejudice** Unreasonable opinions or attitudes based on race, gender, national origin, or another characteristic.

**revolutionize** To change in a significant way.

**rift** An opening in the earth made by the splitting of rock.

**suffrage** The right to vote.

# FOR MORE INFORMATION

**African American Museum of Iowa**

55 12th Avenue SE

Cedar Rapids, IA 52401

(319) 862-2101

Web site: http://www.blackiowa.org

This museum provides exhibits on the history of African Americans in Iowa and offers educational programs for students, including the Children's Oral History Project.

**Amana Colonies Visitors Center**

622 46th Avenue

P.O. Box 310

Amana, IA 52203

(800) 579-2294

Web site: http://www.AmanaColonies.com

Visitors can tour sites in the Amana villages, including historical buildings dating to the 1850s, and see how the people observe a traditional communal way of life.

**Heartland Acres Agribition Center**

2600 Swan Lake Boulevard

Independence, IA 50644

(319) 332-0123

Web site: http://www.heartlandacresusa.com

The center provides interactive exhibits on the past, present, and future of agriculture in Iowa, including an interactive experience for students in a one-room schoolhouse.

**Old Fort Madison**

811 Avenue E

Fort Madison, IA 52627

(319) 372-6318

Web site: http://www.oldfortmadison.com/index.html

Old Fort Madison was the first military outpost on the upper Mississippi River. Visitors can take tours with authentically dressed guides.

**State Historical Society of Iowa Centennial Building**

402 Iowa Avenue

Iowa City, IA 52240-1806

(319) 335-3916

Web site: http://www.iowahistory.org/about/index.html

This organization maintains a historical museum, document archives, and a library.

**Toolesboro Indian Mounds**

Louisa County Conservation Board

Box 261

Wapello, IA 52653

(319) 523-8381

Web site: http://www.iowahistory.org/historic-sites/toolesboro-mounds/index.html

This site contains ancient Paleo-Indian mounds, an education center, and a prairie demonstration plot.

**Western Heritage Trails Center**

3434 Richard Downing Avenue

Council Bluffs, IA 51501

(712) 366-4900

Web site: http://www.iowahistory.org/historic-sites/western-historic-trails/index.html

The Western Heritage Trails Center includes educational exhibits on historic trails, such as Lewis and Clark's trek through the area, and orientation for those wishing to follow this and other historic trails.

## Web Sites

Due to the changing nature of Internet links, Rosen Publishing has developed an online list of Web sites related to the subject of this book. This site is updated regularly. Please use this link to access the list:

http://www.rosenlinks.com/uspp/iapp

# FOR FURTHER READING

Bergman, Marvin, ed. *Iowa History Reader*. Iowa City, IA: University of Iowa Press, 2008.

Bodensteiner, Carol. *Growing Up Country: Memoirs of an Iowa Farm Girl*. Stamford, CT: Rising Sun Press, 2008.

Dyas, Sandra Louise. *Down to the River: Portraits of Iowa Musicians*. Iowa City, IA: Iowa University Press, 2007.

Faldet, David S. *Oneota Flow: The Upper Iowa River and Its People*. Iowa City, IA: Iowa University Press, 2009.

Grant, Roger H. *Railroads Past and Present: Iowa's Railroads—An Album*. Bloomington, IN: Indiana University Press, 2009.

Heynan, Jim. *Sunday Afternoon on the Porch: Reflections of a Small Town in Iowa 1939–1942*. Iowa City, IA: University of Iowa Press, 2007.

Hofsommer, Donovan L., and H. Robert Grant. *Iowa's Railroads: An Album*. Bloomington, IN: Indiana University Press, 2009.

Hoover, Dwight. *Good Day's Work: An Iowa Farm in the Great Depression*. Chicago, IL: Ivan R. Dee Publishers, 2007.

Kalish, Mildred. *Little Heathens: Hard Times and High Spirits on an Iowa Farm During the Great Depression*. New York, NY: Bantam Books, 2008.

Loveless, Leslie. *Children on the Farm: A Postcard Book of Photographs by Pete Wettach*. Iowa City, IA: Iowa University Press, 2004.

McCue, Craig S. *Des Moines 1845–1920*. Charleston, SC: Arcadia Publishing, 2006.

Mutel, Cornelia F. *The Emerald Horizon: The History of Nature in Iowa*. Iowa City, IA: Iowa University Press, 2008.

Pearson, John, Linda Scarth, and Robert Scarth. *Deep Nature: Photographs from Iowa*. Iowa City, IA: University of Iowa Press, 2009.

Smith, Doug. *Postcard History Series: Davenport*. Charleston, SC: Arcadia Publishing, 2007.

Stevick, Richard A. *Growing Up Amish: The Teenage Years*. Baltimore, MD: Johns Hopkins University Press, 2007.

Swieder, Elmer, and Dorothy Swieder. *A Peculiar People: Iowa's Old Order Amish*. Iowa City, IA: University of Iowa Press, 2009.

Whittaker, William. *Frontier Forts of Iowa: Indians, Traders, and Soldiers, 1682–1862*. Iowa City, IA: Iowa University Press, 2009.

# BIBLIOGRAPHY

Andreas, A. T. "History of Iowa Political Record." Illustrated History of Iowa. 1875. Retrieved March 20, 2009 (http://searches.rootsweb.ancestry.com/usgenweb/archives/ia/state/history/andreas/history/413-415.txt).

Iowa Department of Natural Resources Geological Survey. "Landforms." IGSB.com. Retrieved March 2, 2009 (http://www.igsb.uiowa.edu/Browse/landform.htm).

Iowa State Library. "Ola Babcock Miller." StateLibraryOfIowa.org. Retrieved April 1, 2009 (http://www.statelibraryofiowa.org/about/history/miller).

National Mining Association. "Mining in Iowa, 2007." Nma.org. Retrieved March 15, 2009 (http://www.nma.org/pdf/states/econ/ia.pdf).

NebraskaStudies. "The Homestead Act: The Challenge of Living on the Plains." NebraskaStudies.org. Retrieved March 16, 2009 (http://www.nebraskastudies.org/0500/frameset_reset.html?http://www.nebraskastudies.org/0500/stories/0501_0108.html).

Principal Financial Group. "History of the Principal Group." Principal.com. Retrieved April 1, 2009 (http://www.principal.com/about/history/index.htm).

Reschley, Steven D. The Amish on the Iowa Prairie: 1840–1910. Baltimore, MD: Johns Hopkins University Press, 2000.

Schermer, Shirley J., William Green, and James M. Collins. "A Brief Culture History of Iowa." Uiowa.edu. Retrieved March 2, 2009 (http://www.uiowa.edu/~osa/learn/prehistoric/overview.htm).

Schwieder, Dorothy, Thomas Morain, and Lynn Nielsen. Iowa: Past to Present. Ames, IA: Iowa State Press, 2002.

State of Iowa. "Official State of Iowa Web Site." Iowa.gov. Retrieved March 5, 2009 (http://www.iowa.gov/state/main/index.html).

U.S. Census Bureau. "Quick Facts: Iowa." Census.gov. Retrieved March 15, 2009 (http://quickfacts.census.gov/qfd/states/19000.html).

# INDEX

## About the Author

Jeri Freedman has a B.A. from Harvard University. She is the author of more than thirty young adult nonfiction books, many published by Rosen Publishing. Her previous titles include *A Primary Source History of the Colony of Massachusetts*, *Hillary Rodham Clinton: Portrait of a Leading Democrat*, *Library of Genocide: Armenian Genocide*, and *Massachusetts: Past and Present*. Under the name Ellen Foxxe, she is the coauthor of two alternate history science fiction novels.

## Photo Credits

Cover (top left), p. 1 (top left) Yale Collection of Western Americana, Beinecke Rare Book and Manuscript Library; cover (top right), pp. 1 (top right), 28, 30 © AP Images; cover (bottom) © www.istockphoto.com/Mark Halbe; pp. 3, 6, 12, 22, 26, 32, 38, 40 Wikimedia Commons, USDA Photo; p. 4 (top) © GeoAtlas; p. 7 © www.istockphoto.com/Lynn Graesing; p. 9 © Jeff Wignall; pp. 11, 27 Shutterstock.com; p. 13 Smithsonian American Art Museum, Washington, DC/ Art Resource, NY; p. 14 Admission of States and Territorial Acquisition. U.S. Bureau of the Census. Courtesy of the University of Texas Libraries, the University of Texas at Austin; pp. 17, 19, 33 Library of Congress Prints and Photographs Division; p. 23 Ohio Historical Society; pp. 25, 40 Wikimedia Commons; p. 29 Suzanne Opton/Time & Life Pictures/Getty Images; p. 34 Art Rickerby/Time & Life Pictures/Getty Images; p. 37 Lluis Gene/AFP/Getty Images; p. 39 (left) Courtesy of Robesus, Inc.

Designer: Les Kanturek; Photo Researcher: Cindy Reiman